PATHETICALLY POETIC

AMAL JOSEPH

To the weary souls who bend but do not break.

To the dreamers lost in unwritten fates.

To the silent warriors fighting unseen battles.

And to those who wait.

Pathetically, poetically, patiently.

For answers that may never come.

Yet still find meaning in the waiting.

This is for you.

Contents

Contents

Foreword

A multifaceted artist whose creative pursuits span poetry, cinema, literature, and social advocacy. Amal Joseph hails with a postgraduation in Literature. He never fails to bring a profound depth of understanding to the human experience. His work is not confined to any single medium; rather, it is an ongoing dialogue between art and life, exploring the intricate relationships between emotion, intellect, and society.

Poetry possesses a unique ability to excavate the deepest recesses of the human soul, articulating the silent struggles and enlightening the darkness with profound revelation. Amal's verses resonate with the complexities of human existence, capturing the nuances of love, loss, resilience, and introspection. His previous works especially Remembrance resonates a symphony of raw emotion and intellectual depth, seamlessly blending artistry with existential reflection.

This collection of poems transcends mere artistic expression; it serves as an intimate exploration of the human psyche. His verses delve into the realms of heartbreak, perseverance, artistic endeavor, and the unspoken conflicts that shape our inner worlds. From the fallen rulers of history to the silent sufferers of contemporary life, his poetry sheds light on the overlooked and the unheard. With a voice that is both poignant and contemplative, it encapsulates the duality of human nature both fragile and indefatigable, searching yet steadfast.

Through this collection, he extends an invitation to readers to pause, reflect, and find solace within the words. These poems are not a mere amalgamation of phrases; they are the echoes of souls who have endured, fought, and emerged resilient. Each piece carries a profound truth, a narrative yearning to be heard, and an emotional resonance that lingers long after.

As you turn these pages, you'll discover fragments of your own life within them, Amal's words serve as a reminder that even in the darkest moments, there exists an indelible light waiting to be embraced.

Ahmed Al Hamshari

Preface

This is my first book "Pathetically Poetic", born from the quiet battles we fight within, the unspoken emotions that linger in silence, and the raw, unfiltered moments of life that often go unnoticed. These poems reflect love, loss, longing, and the fragile beauty hidden in pain.

We often romanticize the idea of being understood, of finding people who see us for who we truly are. But sometimes, we are loved for the warmth we give, not for the person we are. Sometimes, we carry the weight of unspoken grief and sometimes the world moves on before we are ready. This book is for everyone who has felt unseen, unheard or left behind. For those who love deep, even when it is not returned the same.

Poetry has always been a way to turn pain into art, to give meaning to things that feel meaningless. These words are fragments of moments, reflections of emotions, and echoes of stories that many of us live but never say out loud. If even one poem in this book makes you feel less alone, then this journey is worth it.

Thank you for holding these words in your hands. This book belongs to you.

Amal Joseph

1. THE FALLEN KING

Once he stood where legends rise,
A crown that touched the endless skies.
A kingdom vast, a fate so bright,
A hero bathed in golden light.
But the time is cruel, the tide won't stay,
The winds of fate will sweep away.
His throne now dust, his voice unheard,
His name a long forgotten sword.
He chased his dreams, he held them tight,
Yet watched them vanish into the night.
Like sand that slipped beneath his feet,
A loss too great, a heart's defeat.
Now he walks where echoes fade,
A king undone, a man betrayed.
Yet in his eyes, though torn apart,
Still burns the embers of the heart.

2. THE JOKE WE LIVE

Life's a joke we never tell,
A twisted trick we know too well.
We laugh, we cry, we play our part.
While fate rewrites what's in our heart.
The writer grins, unseen, unknown.
Turning joy to dust and stone.
Dreams dissolve, love fades fast.
Nothing real is meant to last.
Yet still, we hope, still, we try.
Chasing echoes asking why.
But in the end, the stage goes black,
And the joke was always on our back.

3. ART INSTEAD OF ASHES

How many hands have held a pen,
When all they longed for was an end?
How many brushes kissed the page,
To quiet storms, to cage the rage?
The weight too heavy, the nights too long.
Yet ink can turn the pain to song.
A canvas waits, a poem bleeds,
Where silence drowns, the artist pleads.
For some, the bullets stay inside,
Trapped in verses, brushed in light.
A story told, a life held tight,
Saved by art, one more night.

4. THE STORY NEVER BEGAN

Here ends the story that never began,
a tale unwritten, a broken plan.
Dreams unspoken, words held tight.
Fading like stars in the quiet night.
A book once opened, yet never read.
A path once seen, but left unsaid.
Like waves that long to kiss the shore.
Yet drift away, forevermore.

5. LIFE NEVER ENDS

Life never ends when you lose your way,
or when the world feels cold and grey.
It doesn't end when dreams fall apart,
or when pain leaves scars on your heart.
Life goes on, through highs and lows.
Through broken paths and doors that close.
Even when no one understand.
Keep moving forward, life still stands.

6. THE ARTIST'S LEAP

To dream beyond the lines we trace.
To risk the fall, to lose the race.
To chase a light that none can see,
that is where true art must be.
Not every stroke will find its place,
not every note will leave a trace.
Yet still, we try, we dare, we fight.
To turn the dark into the light.
For art is not just what is known,
But what is felt, yet stands alone,
and those who leap with hearts set free
Create the world no eyes can see.

7. DRIFTING INTO SILENCE

A tired soul, with burdens deep,
fought unseen wars, longed for sleep.
The weight he bore, too much to keep,
until the dark called soft and sweet.
Memories danced, both bright and gray,
echoes of laughter, nights turned day.
His weary eyes began to close,
as silence wrapped him in repose.
No anger left, no words to say,
for every heart must lose its way.
With one last breath, he slipped from sight,
a fading star in endless night.
No more battles, no more pain,
no more waiting in the rain.
He let go, light as the breeze,
lost among the endless seas.

8. THE CRITIC'S CHORUS

Not everyone can paint the sky,
or weave a dream that makes hearts fly.
Not all can turn their pain to art,
or craft a world from a broken heart.
Yet voices rise, so loud, so sure,
tearing down what they'll never endure.
No brush in hand, no scars to show,
yet quick to judge what they don't know.
Creation bleeds, but they don't see,
It takes no skill to disagree.
For every artist lost in doubt,
there's a critic screaming out.

9. A CANVAS OF SORROW

At last, he found the perfect way,
a silent path to slip away.
No more waiting, no more cries,
just a final, tired sigh.
He knew they all had reasons deep,
their silent wounds, their grief to keep.
And as his weary eyes grew dim,
the world still swirledbut not for him.
A sky once burned with cobalt bright,
now faded into black and white.
The starry starry night still shines,
the moon still glowed,
yet all he felt was cold and alone.
Sunflowers wilted, fields turned grey,
the colors bled, then slipped away.
And as he fell, the night stood tall.
A masterpiece, his final call.

10. SLOW DOWN

One day, you'll miss this part,
the quiet moments, the racing heart.
The way the sun melts into the sea,
the laughter lost in memories.
You chase the days, you rush, you run,
but time won't wait for anyone.
The little things you push aside,
will be the ones that make you cry.
So breathe it in, don't move so fast,
these fleeting moments never last.
One day, when all is said and done,
you'll wish you hadn't missed this one.

11. MASTER OR SLAVE

The mind is strong, sharp and bright,
It shapes our world in dark and light.
It filters thoughts, false and true,
and guides the things we say and do.
But left alone, it plays its tricks,
it turns our hopes to doubt so quick.
It makes the fear seem big and loud,
and fills our days with heavy clouds.
It lifts us up and slams us down,
will make us smile or let us drown.
A friend, a foe, a force so wide,
the will is ours to shape and guide.
So lead it well, be calm, be wise,
or watch it weave the strangest lies.
For what we think is what we see,
and that alone can set us free.

12. UNTRAVELLED

Regret for the steps we've dared to take,
is lighter than the trail we feared to make.
For paths once chosen, though rough or long,
give us strength, and in them, we belong.
But the roads untraveled, the dreams unspoken,
leave hearts in sorrow, and spirits broken.
Better the journey, with all its toils,
than the quiet ache of a life unlived in life.

13. THE ARTIST'S REBELLION

An artist must break, must tear apart,
the walls that cage a dreaming heart.
For art is wild, it will not stay,
it carves its own, untamed.
No borrowed lines, no measured mold,
no echoes of the past retold.
Creation lives where rules are none,
where chains are smashed.
A rebel's fire, a spirit free,
That is where true art must be.
Not bound by fear, nor shaped by hands,
but born where courage dares to stand.

14. SHADOWS OF MEMORY

The memories I buried deep and low,
are the ones that in the darkness glow.
No matter how I turn away,
they beg to stay, but left alone.
I teach myself to walk ahead,
to silence echoes in my head.
Yet in the night, they call my name.
The past I fled, but left untamed.

15. THE SMILE HE NEVER KNEW

He laughed by day, he wept by night,
A burning star with fading light.
A masterpiece the world admired,
yet lost within, bruised and tired.
He played the role, he wore the mask,
a hollow joy, a fragile task.
For those who saw beyond his eyes,
Knew his laughter was all a lie.
From childhood days since years gone by,
He never learned to truly smile.
So in each picture he posed,
A man unsure, a heart half-closed.
And when no hope was left to find,
he left his colors far behind.
A soul too bright, a heart too wild,
Yet never once a real smile.

16. STAND ALONE

When the crowds scream, lost in rage,
be the calm, shift the page.
When they trade the truth for bitter lies,
Must hold your ground, never compromise.
Madness spreads like wildfire bright,
Blinding reason, dimming light.
In the storm, let courage guide,
Not the reckless, thrashing raging tide.
Let them fall, let them astray,
But keep your soul, don't fade away.
For when the mob has burned it all,
Only those who stood will stand tall.

17. THE UNFORGIVEN

If betrayal could be erased,
the devil would find his rightful place.
No flames to burn, no endless fall,
just open gates, justice withdrawn.
Once he stood where angels sang,
golden light where echoes rang.
But trust was lost, a bond was torn,
and from that loss, a curse was born.
He cried for mercy, called His name,
but heaven's door remained sealed.
For some betrayals cut too deep,
but some mistakes are ours to keep.
So here he stands, forever exiled,
a fallen soul, a ruined hand.
For even grace must draw a line,
not all wounds can heal with time.

18. WHEN DREAMS ARE GONE

One day, his dreams will count to none,
no battles left, no race to run.
He'll sit in darkness, lost in space,
a fading soul, an empty place.
No words to speak, no thoughts to share,
just vacant eyes and hollow stare.
Time will slip, the days will blur,
a life once bright, now just a blur.
And then, one day, he'll disappear,
no name to call, no trace, no tear.
The world will turn, as it always must,
his story fading into dust.

19. THE RUINED CITY

The battles within him raged and fell,
defeat met him at every spell.
No matter how hard he tried to stand,
fate slipped like grains of sand.
Words struck sharp from every side,
wounds unseen, yet deep inside.
Rather than fight a war in vain,
he chose the name too numb for pain.
The Joy had long walked away,
laughed at him, then gone astray.
As each battle slipped from sight,
His heart became the land,
ruined by the war, lost to the night.

20. THE DYSTOPIA WE MADE

Why write of cities torn and lost,

when we live in the one that hides the cost?

Why dream of futures dark and cold,

when the truth is already told?

The air is heavy, filled with sighs,

dreams are stolen, wrapped in lies.

Towers rise, yet hearts still break,

we chase a life that feels unreal.

No stories nor fear,

the end we dread is already here.

A world so lost, yet none will see,

a cage we built and called it free.

21. THE FINAL REST

A weary soul, with burdens deep,
fought silent wars, began to weep.
The nights grew cold, the days unkind,
no peace to see, no light to blind.
Black and white, the past replays,
the laughter lost, the smiles decays.
His heavy eyes, the world grew dim,
a fading tune, a whispered hymn.
No blame he cast, rage never stayed,
the heart holds wounds that never fade.
With one last sigh, the pain set free,
he drifts into eternity.

22. A QUIET EXIT

That's how I died, the most beautiful way,
not in the dark, nor lost in the grey.
Not by the blade, nor swallowed by sea,
but by the love that was never meant to be.
It slipped like dusk through trembling hands,
a sun that set on promised lands.
Not torn away, nor ripped apart,
but fading gently from the heart.
I smiled, I sighed, I let it go,
a quiet death, so painful, so slow.
No cries, no pain, no last goodbyes,
just love that lived, then learned to die.

23. THE SILENT WAR

In their eyes, a sloth he seemed,
a drifting soul, a man who dreamt.
Yet none could see the war inside,
the silent screams, the nights he wept.
Each defeat, weighed so deep,
a burden far too hard to keep.
Easier to wear their scornful names,
than fight a war they'd never claim.
Joy, a flicker lost in time.
The days stretched long, a heavy climb.
His mind, a city, walls so tall,
hiding battles none recall.
Echoes haunt, they'd never fade,
a fortress bruised, a heart betrayed.
Misunderstood, left in the darkness,
the silent war, alone he fought.

24. THE COST OF A CHAPTER

To craft a tale, one pays the price.
In sleepless nights and sacrifice.
The pages filled with love and strife,
the highs, the lows, the vitals of life.
The words are inked in quiet cries,
some in hope that never dies.
Sometimes, ere the tale is through,
a soul is lost to make it true.
For every tale, bright or grim,
holds fading voices, echoes dim.
And when the final page is turned,
we leave behind the life we burnt.

25. THE VILLIAN'S TALE

The hero stands, the tale is told,

a savior brave, with a heart of gold.

Yet in his light, the shadows grow.

And I'm the monster they portrayed.

He writes the story, sets the stage,

and paints my fate in lines of rage.

No one asks what brought me here,

or why my name is one they fear.

Was I the monster, born in hate?

Or shaped by hands that sealed my fate?

The villain stays, the hero shines,

when truth is drawn in scripted lines.

26. FOR THE ONE'S LEFT BEHIND.

To the ones left out, the souls unheard.
The hearts that ache where none can see.
Never less nor to be wrong,
seeking the place where you belong.
Friendships fade, people leave,
but love will find, come what may.
One day, we'll stand where kindness stays.
Where laughter lingers, warmth remains.
Hold on tight, don't dim your light,
your worth will shine so bright.
The right hearts will find, just be patient,
and love you for the soul you were always been.

Epilogue

I am not a poet by virtue, nor do I claim to be one. These words were never meant to be a book; just thoughts scribbled in my notes. Fragments of emotions, moments of silence and echoes of thoughts left unsaid.

My words are not about polished verses or perfect rhymes. It's about the ones who fell yet refused to break, the ones whose voice were drowned out by the noise of the world. It's for those who were left unremembered, unrepresented, never given a place in the grand stories of our times.

From "The Fallen King" to "For The One's Left Behind", these poems are for those who walk unnoticed through the streets of modern life. The dreamers, the loners, the ones who carry the weights of past battles unseen. This is not just about poetry; it is a quiet rebellion, a reminder that even in the forgotten corners left unnoticed, their stories still matter. If you have found a single line that felt like yours, these words have found their place.

For the unheard, the unremembered.

You're welcome.

Amal Joseph